GREENHOUSE
GARDENING FOR BEGINNERS

The Complete Step-by-Step Guide to Start Growing Your Own Vegetables and Fruits All-Year-Round by Building an Eco-Friendly Greenhouse and Hydroponic Garden

Written by:

Aaron Farmer

AARON FARMER

Table Of Contents

Introduction

Greenhouse gardening is not a contemporary idea. The technology and system date back to the Roman Realm. The earliest reference to the greenhouse gardening concept is directed to the Roman Emperor Tiberius. He demanded to have Armenian cucumbers every day at the royal table. Royal gardeners thought of ways to obey the emperor's order. They found out that by creating a sealed enclosure, they can control temperatures, humidity, and light exposure required by cucumbers for growth and fruit-bearing. They used a special system very similar to that of modern greenhouses.

During those times, having a greenhouse was limited to the wealthy. By the 19th century, greenhouses became more of an academic need. Universities put up large greenhouses, designed to hold several rare species of plants. During this time, Western civilization was starting to explore the other side of the world. Explorers and scholars were bringing back a lot of specimens from these exotic places, most of which were pretty interesting, but cannot tolerate cold climates. In order to preserve the plants in their full, natural bloom, greenhouses were the likely solution.

Greenhouse gardening can then be well-defined as the discipline of growing plants in a founded building by means of materials typically translucent or transparent such that the plants are provided with controlled favorable environmental conditions. Plants that are cultivated in greenhouses receive protection against conditions like soil erosion, harsh weather, violent rain and storm, plant pathogens, etc. This system of gardening is also called glasshouse or hothouse by some growers, and the major reason for setting it up is probably to secure a considerable quantity of water vapor and heat to maintain humidity and proper temperature in the greenhouse.

The technology of greenhouse gardening serves as a viable solution to bridge the gap between the increasing world population and the increasing demand. The gap was created as a result of the urbanization of certain countries involving the construction of roads, etc., and also industrialization, which has inevitably made much arable land uncultivable.

The growth of plants under adverse weather conditions will eventually become stunted, this is why plants grow better in a greenhouse, although the growth of plants in the greenhouse is influenced by humidity, ventilation, light, and also the rate of plant watering. The environmental condition of the greenhouse can be classified into the physical environment—which includes water, light, temperature, etc.—and the biotic environment—which includes insects, microorganisms, etc.

Humidity levels above 85% in the greenhouse should, by all means, be avoided as this tends to cause more harm than good to the plants. When the humidity level in the greenhouse is too much, the plants become weak and flaccid, in which case the humid air needs to be exhausted. The need for the presence of fresh air in the greenhouse cannot be overemphasized as it encourages photosynthesis, pollination, and pest prevention. Plants generally require about 6–12 hours of light daily, therefore, in a situation where the plants in the greenhouse are not exposed to enough natural light, artificial light should be incorporated and adequately so. Also, too much supply of water in the greenhouse is just as dangerous to the plants as the lack of water supply. But factors such as growing medium, temperature, plant size, etc. contribute greatly to the determination of the amount of watering required by the plant. After you have selected the location to set up your greenhouse, the building can be self-built by placing an order for an already made "Do-It-Yourself" greenhouse kit. Setting things up in most cases is simple but in some other cases, it can also be a bit complex. For starters, not much high-tech equipment is required to practice greenhouse gardening. The greenhouse technique can be practiced simply or expanded depending on the scale of production intended.

CHAPTER 1:

The Basics of Greenhouse

It was circa 30 A.D., and Emperor Tiberius needed more cucumbers.

More specifically, he needed one cucumber a day, according to his physicians, to help him with an ailment. This is why Roman engineers and gardeners had to find a way to maintain continuous production of cucumbers, which would not have been a challenge if not for the fact that they had to provide these cucumbers specifically for the emperor all year round.

So, they decided to brainstorm: How does one grow the same plant throughout the year?

You see, cucumbers flourish during warm and moist seasons. This means the engineers had to find a way to raise cucumbers during the snowy winters. Yes, it did snow in the Roman Empire. Not everything in Rome was about politics and gladiator fights on a hot and sunny day.

To solve the problem for the emperor, the engineers used a wheeled cart to carry the cucumbers and placed the cart under the sun. This gave the cucumbers the necessary warmth they needed. When night arrived (or when it was winter), a special cover made from frames coated with transparent materials housed the cucumbers, keeping them warm.

By doing this, the engineers helped the emperor dig his teeth into some delicious cucumbers. After all, a cucumber a day keeps the physicians away (or those backstabbing politicians away; it was Rome after all).

But the point I am trying to make here is that greenhouses are not a recent invention. They have been part of human history for centuries. This fact is not so surprising. After all, agriculture developed thousands of years before humans began to write. It would not be a stretch to imagine that someone figured out how to produce crops at any time during the year.

Greenhouses are mostly transparent structures where plants are grown. You can typically find them in cold regions like parts of Canada, Finland, and Greenland, but they are not confined to those countries. The transparent covering is usually made of glass and allows sunlight to pass through during the day. During the nighttime, the glass traps the heat inside, continuing to keep the plants warm despite the temperatures outside.

It is an ingenious invention that makes use of physics. Today, you can find the name associated with climate change.

Greenhouses themselves are not responsible for climate change, but the name is used to describe the process that causes temperatures to increase on the Earth's surface; the greenhouse effect. In this effect, gases such as carbon dioxide trap the heat from the sun, just like the glass roofs of greenhouses. People who are unaware of the functions of greenhouses often wonder if the structures cause harm to the environment. But research has shown that these glassed structures are indeed environmentally friendly.

Benefits of a Greenhouse

Garden of Eden

Some plants grow well during the summer, utilizing the abundant sunlight available. Then there are those plants that grow well during the winter, finding the cold weather more comfortable. Greenhouses help maintain a stable temperature within their facility, whether it is in the middle of the summer or during freezing winters.

Plants that are subjected to abrupt changes in temperatures do not grow healthily. They are at risk of losing their nutrients and even growing stunted. With greenhouses, you are providing a controlled environment for plants and herbs to not merely grow, but thrive. You can even add specific features to your greenhouse—such as ventilation systems—to keep conditions just the way you, or your plants, like them. This becomes essential for growing certain types of crops, herbs, flowers, or plants. For example, you can start raising fruits like tomatoes. Yes, they are fruits. Science has helped settle the age-long debate about whether tomatoes belong in the fruit category or not.

Variety Is Spice!

With the right conditions, there are many plants that you can grow in a greenhouse. Do you need some vegetables? Get your greenhouse ready for vegetables (and fruits) such as tomatoes, peppers, and even cucumbers (whether you are an emperor/empress who needs them daily or not). Are you interested in raising crops? Because you can work with options such as broccoli, lettuce, peas, and carrots. From warm-seasoned crops to cold-season crops; from ornamentals to even tropical flowers, you can grow a plethora of plants right in your backyard!

You can use what you produce in your greenhouse to decorate your house or create your garden. When you perfect your techniques, you can even sell your products at the local market. And if you do not want to grow your plants to sell them, that's okay, too.

Protection Detail

When you are raising crops and plants, pests become a common enemy. From ants to flies, wasps, aphids, and beetles, crops and plants might come under attack numerous times during the year. Each country in the world is home to numerous pests. However, some creatures are found abundantly in one region or country and less (and sometimes never) in another location.

For example, tobacco whiteflies are common pests in regions such as Asia, Africa, and Europe, but are not typically found in North America. However, fall armyworms are found in regions such as North and South American, Africa, and certain parts of Europe.

Regardless of where you are and what pest plagues your region, the crops and plants in your region face a threat from these creatures.

Using greenhouses, you are giving plants a safe place to grow and in turn, they reward you in many ways. While it is true that pests are capable of attacking greenhouses as well, you have a better chance of getting rid of them.

Don't Bug Me!

You do not need pests to ruin plants. Even insects that are commonly found in practically every region on the planet can also cause a lot of harm.

Whether they are ants or houseflies, they are capable of causing much destruction to plants and crops. One of the ways that they can do this is by directly attacking the plants.

Another method is by causing harm indirectly. Insects can do this by spreading infections or diseases to the crops. These diseases can be viral, bacterial, or even fungal. By simply affecting a few crops, insects can ensure that the diseases spread to nearby plants, which in turn carry the infection further.

Wherever these insects cause damage, they often multiply and grow in the same area. This prevents farmers and gardeners from growing crops in that location again. Eventually, the insects and their offspring have to be dealt with (which is a painstakingly lengthy process) before growing any produce.

Greenhouses provide you a solution to the insect problem in the form of raised beds. You will learn more about these structures later, but essentially, they are containers that hold plants. In the event of an insect infestation, you can easily clean out the raised beds and plant crops again.

Energy Efficient

Greenhouses use sunlight, for the most part. This creates a natural lighting and heating system for the plants, which is in turn essential for the process known as photosynthesis. In this process, the plants convert carbon dioxide into essential nutrients using the light from the sun.

Furthermore, light is also involved in a process called transpiration. Think of this process as the way plants breathe, and it usually occurs during the early hours of the day. In this process, light enters tiny pores that are present on the surface of leaves and allows the plant to receive gases from the environment.

All of this is essential to keep your plants and crops healthy.

What makes using greenhouses beneficial is that by using natural light, you are reducing the reliance on electrically supplied lighting. When this happens, you are removing the high consumption of energy from the equation. People have this notion that greenhouses tap into a lot of electricity for maintenance. This is not true unless you choose to add certain features to the greenhouse that require power. While greenhouses do consume electricity, you can design yours in such a way that it minimizes electricity usage.

With greenhouses, you are mainly dependent on what nature is already providing you in abundance.

Planting Some Zen in Your Life

You read that right. Greenhouses help you relieve stress and bring a sense of calm into your life. This might sound like a metaphysical or spiritual approach to looking at greenhouses. However, science has some answers about why you feel relaxed inside greenhouses.

According to the National Center for Biotechnology Information, engaging with indoor plants has led to the reduction of not just psychological, but physiological stress. By conducting a simple experiment involving young adults, they noticed that participants of the experiment began to show feelings of comfort and calm after working with indoor plants.

CHAPTER 2:

Planning Your Greenhouse

Type, Location, and Size

First, when starting the process of planning your greenhouse, you need to make sure that you have chosen the type of greenhouse that you are going to build. This will make the rest of the decisions that you are about to make much easier.

Next, you will need to choose where your greenhouse will be located. Typically, the south side of your home is the best place to put a greenhouse. This is because it will get the best and most sunlight in this location. Be sure when choosing your location, though, that there will be nothing that blocks the sun from reaching your greenhouse. For example, if your yard is bordered by tall trees and the south side of your property never sees the sun, then your property is an exception from the fact that the south side is typically the best for greenhouses. If you do not have space on the south side, it is also okay to choose a different location. You want to ensure that you get to create a perfect greenhouse—no matter what its location is. The most important thing to consider is that space receives a decent amount of direct sunlight throughout the day.

You also need to figure out how big you want your greenhouse to be. You will want to think about the big picture while you are making this choice. How many plants you would like to grow this year is one thing to consider, but you will also want to think about how many plants you could see yourself growing 10 years down the road. You will probably want to build your greenhouse big enough to fit your dream garden so that later on you do not have to regret making it too small. You also need to consider the space that you have available when you are making this decision. Do you have enough space in your designated location for a large greenhouse or do you need to build a smaller structure?

Airflow

Let's start looking into how to design the inside of your greenhouse practically and functionally by looking at airflow. Airflow is needed to ensure that the plants get what they need. Plants breathe in a way that is the opposite of humans. Humans breathe in oxygen and exhale out carbon dioxide.

Humans need fresh air to supply oxygen where they are breathing, because breathing back in the carbon dioxide that they breathed out will do no good for sustaining life.

This same principle is true with plants. Plants need carbon dioxide in the air so that they can breathe it in. When they breathe out, they release oxygen. Oxygen is not good for sustaining the life of the plants. Because of this, the air in greenhouses needs to be circulated just like it is naturally outside so that plants are breathing in the things that they actually need for them to survive. Airflow in greenhouses is achieved mainly through the use of fans. There are quite a few options based on the types of fans and the location of fans that you will need to plant out, however. Each of these options comes with its own specific set of benefits. You will need to decide what will work best in your structure and for the plants that you are most wanting to grow. Next, let's look into the different types of fans that you can choose from:

- The first type of fan that is commonly found in greenhouses is called a basket fan. Basket fans are very powerful and have wide slots. They are strong fans, so they can circulate air well, but when they are used in sequences, they do not always provide a uniform stream of air. This can cause some plants to get a lot of airflow and others to get none at all.
- Shrouded fans are an option as well. They can provide more consistent airflow to all plants. They are also great for conserving energy, so if you are looking to "go green" with your greenhouse, shrouded fans could be a great choice.

After you choose a fan type, you will have to decide if you want your airflow to be vertical or horizontal. Both methods have their good points and not so good points:

- Vertical airflow, for example, helps to ensure that the temperature of the greenhouse stays even throughout the entire structure from top to bottom.
- Horizontal airflow is better at making sure that the humidity levels are consistent among every area of plants in the greenhouse.

Cooling and Heating

Next, let's look into cooling and heating. We know that these are two of the most important factors to look into when designing a new greenhouse. The purpose of a greenhouse is actually to extend the growing season of your plants and your garden, and one of the biggest ways that they can do this is through temperature control. When you can control the temperature of your greenhouse, you do not need to rely on the natural climate in your area for the health and success of your plants. Let's look into some things that you can do to your greenhouse so that you can control the temperature well:

- First, let's look into greenhouse heating techniques. Make sure that it is in a location that gets a lot of sunlight and that it is made from a material that allows heat to enter inside. You can also make sure that your greenhouse has no cracks that could let breezes of cold air come in.

- You could also consider using solar panels on top of your greenhouse to collect energy for heat so that you could continue along the environmentally friendly path that your greenhouse idea started.

- When you live in a cold area, you will need to plan for these things during the design process. Consider installing a heater or solar panels right away so that your plants are never hurt by painfully cold temperatures.

- The first thing to try when your greenhouse begins to get too warm is to cool it down with the fans that you use for air circulation. If this also does not work, you can buy a cover for your greenhouse to give your plants a break from the heat that the sun provides them with.

- When designing your greenhouse, you will want to make sure that you have the option to use these methods if you live in a very warm climate. You can consider walls that can be rolled up partially to allow for ventilation. You will want to make sure that your design includes fans. You may even want to consider having a cover ready for the days that you know your greenhouse will get too much sun and therefore too much heat.

Humidity

Next, let's look at the humidity in your greenhouse. If your greenhouse is too humid, you will want to make sure that you are using the horizontal fan method. This helps to circulate the air directly around the plants so that the humidity does not sit in them for too long. Another way to design your greenhouse so that humidity is never an issue is to have flooring that drains well. This will make sure that there is never excess water in your greenhouse that could lead to too much humidity in the air.

The flooring of your greenhouse is also important. As we mentioned earlier, it is important to have floor drains if you think that humidity is going to be a problem because of the climate that you live in.

Besides this, though, there are many things to keep in mind when choosing a greenhouse flooring material. Let's look into the different types of materials that are commonly used in greenhouse flooring as well as what each different choice is good for.

Floors

Next, let's look into the different types of greenhouse floors as well as what each different type is good for. One popular flooring type for a greenhouse is concrete.

The concrete is easy to walk on and easy to keep clean. It is also easy to slope so that you can get good drainage in your building. To have a concrete floor, you will probably have to have a concrete slab made before you build your greenhouse.

CHAPTER 3:

Overview of Different Types of Greenhouse

T he type of greenhouse structure determines the productivity and efficiency of your gardening activities. New to greenhouse gardening. It will make it easier for beginners to choose the right structure based on their needs.

As a plant grower, you need to understand the efficiency of plant production and control of environmental conditions. Choosing the right greenhouse will enable you to create an ideal working environment for your vegetables, herbs, and fruits. It also allows you to create a plant growing plan that ensures you meet the specific needs of your crop.

These designs are based on the materials, shape, utility, and construction process. Most designs are classified as:

- **Attached**
  - Lean-to greenhouse structure
  - Even span greenhouse structure

- **Freestanding or Independent Structures**
  o Uneven span greenhouse structure
  o A-frame greenhouse structure
  o Quonset greenhouse structure
  o Gothic arch greenhouse structure
- **Gutter Connected Structures**
  o Ridge and furrow type greenhouse
  o Sawtooth greenhouse

Lean-To Greenhouse Structure

Just like the name suggests, a lean-to greenhouse structure is built leaning on the side of another structure. It is classified as an attached greenhouse structure, meaning that the roof of the greenhouse connects to another building. You don't have to build all the four walls of the greenhouse because, by design, it shares one of its walls.

The structure should face the right direction to obtain adequate sunlight exposure. It should mostly face the southern side and the roof should have the best covering material. a lean-to greenhouse is ideal for growing herbs and vegetables.

This structure was common during the Victorian period, and it is one of the traditional structures available. Building against the wall offers additional support to the structure, making it strong and wind-resistant. The wall also absorbs heat during the day and releases that heat at night, which helps to maintain the temperature of the greenhouse during cool nights.

If you're planning to use a lean-to structure, you need to put the height of the structure into consideration together with any metal base. This ensures the ridges do not come in contact with any windows or drainage pipes in the principal building.

Advantages

- **Cost-effective:** This type of structure is less expensive compared to other greenhouse structures.
- **Minimize building materials:** The design is built against an existing wall, thus saving you on building material for four walls. It also minimizes roofing material requirements, since the design makes the best use of sunlight.
- **Resources:** The structure is constructed close to water, electricity, and heat.

Disadvantages

- **Limited sunlight:** Building a lean-to structure against a house or garage limits the amount of sunlight to only the three walls. It will also have limited light, ventilation, and minimum temperature control.
- **Limited to the building orientation:** The best structure should be on the southern exposure. The

height of the building or the supporting wall affects the design and the size of the greenhouse.

- **Temperature control:** It is difficult to control the temperature of the structure because the wall absorbs a lot of heat during the day and distributes it for use on cool nights. Some translucent covers lose heat more rapidly, making it difficult to control the heat.

- **Foundation:** You need to build a strong foundation for this greenhouse to last long, especially when using glass with the lean-to greenhouse.

Even Span Greenhouse Structure

Even span is another attached type of greenhouse, and it attaches more to promote plant growth. This standard structure is attached to a building, and its roof is made of two slopes of equal length and width. The structure can allow you to plant two to three rows, with two side benches and a wide bench at the center.

Even span design is more flexible and has curved eaves to boost their shape. Due to its great shape, there is plenty of air circulation in the greenhouse, thus making it easier to control temperatures. You also need to have an extra heating system especially when the structure is far away from a heated building. The heating system is especially important during the winter season.

Advantages

- It provides enough space for the growth of plants and vegetables.
- It is easier and more economic in construction, making it the most popular design for a greenhouse.
- You have easy access to water and electricity within the building.

Disadvantages

- High cost of construction and heating system compared to the lean-to structure.
- Reduced sunlight exposure due to the shadow from the house it is attached to.

Uneven Span Greenhouse Structure

In this structure, the roof is made of uneven or unequal width. The greenhouse is constructed such that one rooftop slope is longer than the other, making the design suitable for hilly terrain or when you want to take advantage of solar energy.

Uneven slopes are laid so the steeper angles of the greenhouse face to the south.

Uneven greenhouses are no longer used because most farmers prefer setting up a greenhouse on flat land.

Advantages

- As mentioned, this greenhouse is in a hilly area.
- There is no obstruction of sunlight because the longer slope allows for more sunlight to enter the structure. The longer side also faces south, thus maximizing heat from the sun's rays.

Disadvantages

- It can be costly compared to even span greenhouses.
- They require more support on the slanted roof.
- Uneven span greenhouses usually need a lot of maintenance on the roof after some time.
- Too much solar can penetrate the greenhouse if the uneven-span greenhouse is located in areas close to the equator.

A-Frame Greenhouse Structure

The A-frame greenhouse style is one of the most common designs.

The structure is simple to set and it is ideal for a small backyard garden.

To form the A-frame, you would attach the roof and sidewalls of the greenhouse together, which forms a triangular-like shape.

Most A-framed greenhouses use translucent, polycarbonate material, which helps to eliminate the cost of having to buy glass material.

Most A-framed greenhouses are laid down in an open field or the backyard facing the southern side.

Advantages

- It maximizes the use of space along the side walls.
- Simple and straightforward to construct.
- Conservative structure style, using minimal material

Disadvantages

- It has poor air circulation at the corners of the triangle.
- Its narrow sidewalls limit the overall use of the greenhouse.

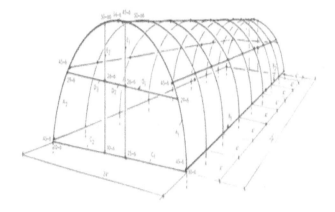

Quonset Greenhouse Structure/ Hoop-House Structure

The Quonset design has a curved roof or arched rafters, and its design is similar to the military-hut style. The circular band in the structure's style is made of aluminum or PVC pipes, while the rooftop is made of plastic sheeting. The sidewalls of the design are set low, however, so there is not a whole lot of headroom. The hoops on the rooftop ensure there is no accumulation of snow and water on the top.

You would build this type of greenhouse in an open field or backyard with the structure facing the southern side.

Advantages

- Easy to build and one of the cheapest designs due to the use of plastic sheeting.
- Its design allows rainwater and melted snow to run off.
- Suitable for a small plant growing space.

Disadvantages

- Limited storage space.
- Its frame design is not as sturdy as the A-frame design.
- As stated, there is less headroom in the structure.

Gothic Arch Greenhouse Structure

Gothic arch has a nice aesthetic and is one of the most visually pleasing designs available. T

he walls of the structure are bent over a frame, forming a pointed roof-like structure.

The design requires less material to construct, as there is no need for trusses.

Most Gothic arch designs are made of plastic sheeting, and its design allows you to construct a large greenhouse where you can plant various products in rows.

Advantages

- The design has minimum heat exposure, thus making it easy to conserve heat.
- Plastic sheeting reduces the cost of construction.
- It has a simple and efficient design that allows rainwater and snow to flow away.

Disadvantages

- Not enough headroom and the design has a low sidewall height, which limits the storage of the greenhouse design.

Ridge and Furrow Greenhouse Structure

This type of design uses two or more A-framed design structures connected to one another along the roof eave length. The eaves offer more protection and act as a furrow to allow melted snow or rainwater to flow away.

There are no sidewalls on the structure, which creates more ventilation in the greenhouse. It also reduces automation cost and fuel consumption, since only a small wall area is exposed where the heat can escape.

Ridge and furrow greenhouse structure is ideal for growing vegetables, and they're mostly used in Europe, Canada, the Netherlands, and Scandinavian countries.

Advantages

- Ideal for large-scale farming, and it's easy to expand this type of greenhouse.
- Provides more ventilation into the greenhouse.
- Requires few materials for construction because of its lack of sidewalls.
- Requires little energy to cool and heat.

Disadvantages

- Lack of a proper water drainage system will damage your plants.

- Although the design has no side walls, shadows from the gutters can prevent sunlight from entering the greenhouse.

Sawtooth Greenhouse Structure

This type of greenhouse structure is similar to the ridge and furrow; however, Sawtooth offers more natural ventilation. This is due to its natural ventilation flow path developed as a result of the Sawtooth design. The roof provides 25% of the total ventilation to the greenhouse, and opening the Sawtooth vents will ensure there is continuous airflow into the greenhouse. This makes it easy to control the temperatures and ensure the plants are in good climatic conditions for their growth.

Advantages

- Sawtooth arches provide excellent light transmission into the greenhouse.
- A high rooftop allows for natural heat ventilation and airflow in the greenhouse.
- Excellent structure for both warm and cold climatic conditions.
- Simple and strong greenhouse structure.
- Has a large farming area.

Cold Frame Greenhouse Structure

A cold frame is ideal for greenhouse gardening in your backyard and allows you to plant plants and vegetables at any time. It is one of the cheapest and simplest greenhouses you can set up. In cold frame gardening, you place a glass or plastic sheeting as the cover of the greenhouse structure, which will help in protecting your crops from frost, snow, rain, wind, or low temperatures.

A cold frame greenhouse is suitable for planting cold-loving plants like broccoli, cauliflower, and cabbage among others.

Based on your budget, you can go for glass, polycarbonate, or plastic sheeting material to construct the greenhouse. The design requires a few openings to allow the ventilation of heat into the greenhouse.

Hotbed Greenhouse

The hotbed structure acts as a miniature type of greenhouse that traps heat from solar radiation. This greenhouse can provide a favorable environment for plants that need a lot of heat like tomatoes, eggplants, and peppers.

If you want to extend the growing season, you can use hotbeds to provide the right weather conditions for your crops. Whether during winter, summer, or spring, there is always a family of vegetables, fruits, or herbs you can grow.

CHAPTER 4:

Buying a New or a Used Greenhouse

Buying a new greenhouse is just too expensive for many. They aren't cheap and the cost means a lot of people do not buy one.

A good option is to buy a used greenhouse either through eBay, Freecycle, Gumtree, or local ads. Often these are a fraction of the price of a new greenhouse, and you can even find greenhouses for free! Some people, when they move into a new home, find a greenhouse they don't want and will offer it for free to someone willing to come and take it away.

When buying a used greenhouse, you will be expected in many cases to disassemble the greenhouse yourself. Take lots of pictures of the greenhouse before you take it apart, as it will help you to put it back together again. Make notes on any non-standard panes and where they belong. Plenty of pictures from all angles is the easiest way to do this.

Taking a greenhouse down and reassembling it will be a two-person job, so you need to find yourself a helper to make the job easier.

You will need some tools to take down the greenhouse, including a wide selection of spanners, both open and closed-ended. You will also need a variety of screwdrivers, both flat and cross-head, and also large ones. A ratchet spanner will help you a lot and make things easier. A good pair of pliers can also help with the more stubborn bolts.

I would also recommend a can of WD-40® to help ease rusted bolts as well as a junior hacksaw for those exceptionally stubborn bolts.

You should wear gloves, particularly while moving the glass; otherwise, you will end up with plenty of cuts on your hands.

Ideally, you will want to disassemble the greenhouse on a dry day because doing it in the rain is unpleasant (trust me on this) and much harder as everything becomes slippery.

It is worthwhile labeling parts as you take them apart as it will help you a lot when putting them back together. If you can get a van, then you don't have to take the greenhouse down completely. You can just break it into the front, rear, and side panels and the two halves of the roof and fit them in the van. It will save you a lot of work if you can do it this way!

Most used greenhouses will be on the smaller side, usually 8x6' or thereabouts. If you want a larger greenhouse, then just get two smaller greenhouses and join them together!

As with any greenhouse, the first thing you need to do is build a base following instructions. Just make sure that the base is square (measure the diagonals) and level (use a spirit level that is at least 3 feet long).

Before you dive headlong into assembling your greenhouse, you need to sort out all the bits and pieces. Ensure you have enough nuts and bolts and that those you have are usable. Sometimes they can be rusted, or the thread stripped, so you will want to have enough to hand. The last thing you want to do is to go halfway when you find that important parts are missing. Buy from most home improvement stores or online.

Also, make sure you have plenty of glass clips as these often go missing or get broken when taking a greenhouse to pieces.

Make sure all the glass pieces are present, and none are broken. You cannot assemble your greenhouse without all the panes, as that will make it extremely susceptible to wind damage.

Check the weather forecast before you start building your greenhouse as doing it in the rain is no fun and doing it in high winds is positively dangerous!

Sort the struts out, group them into each of the sides and the roof. This allows you to check you have all the pieces and then assemble each side before you put it all together.

After the frame is assembled, you need to start placing the glass in place. This is best done from the top down because you can get around the greenhouse better without glass in the frame beneath you. This is when you realize that your glazing clips are broken, twisted, or even missing, so buy a bag or two before you start! Remember that glass doesn't bend, so you need to be careful putting it in. An 8x6' greenhouse can end up using up to 200 of these clips!

It is also worthwhile buying some extra rubber seals that the glass fits into. Invariably when taking a greenhouse to pieces, these will break or get lost.

Buy all the spare parts you need before you start reassembling the greenhouse. It will make your life much easier.

Just remember to be careful when reassembling your greenhouse. The glass can and will break, so transport it with care. It isn't a race, so just take your time and make sure you have someone to help you!

CHAPTER 5:

Pros/Cons of a Greenhouse

G reenhouses are very popular, especially among those who want to have things growing all year long, but they come with disadvantages as well. It's important to understand the possible downsides to have a greenhouse. This will help you to come to the best decision for you.

Cons

Lack of Pollination

Even if you think you have the best control over your plants inside your greenhouse, some plants will carry pests like whiteflies that could quickly spread to all your other plants. This could sabotage most of your vegetables and plants you are growing. You also need to realize that natural pollinators aren't going to be able to get to your crops. This might be a huge disadvantage for some of the fruits and vegetables that you are growing.

Expensive to Operate

To make sure your greenhouse is being used for its maximum output; you are going to need to invest in supplies that can make sure your crops have a great lifespan. If you install a cheap plastic film to keep heat in, it might be perfectly fine. But if you use more expensive glass windows, they will last longer, and you will be able to ventilate your greenhouse when you open them. When heating your greenhouse, you might notice a large increase in your monthly electric bills if you use heaters of any kind.

Pros

Lowers Threats

When you grow your plants inside a greenhouse, you can prevent predators from eating your crops. With a greenhouse, you are always in control of what comes in and out of your greenhouse. Plus, this kind of environment will protect your crops from disease, pests, and the weather. You can minimize the risks of insects and pests that could kill your plants.

Larger Variety

When you get your produce at a grocery store or supermarket, you have to pay their price because they rely on production methods, availability, and demand. Different types of produce have various growing seasons. But, if you build your greenhouse, you will have an opportunity to have a large variety of produce throughout the year. By doing this, you can create a more extensive assortment of products for consumers when markets have a lower supply. Greenhouses allow you to grow new vegetables or flowers that don't normally thrive where you live. Because of this, you might provide the best growing environment for whatever crop you decide to grow.

Extended Growing Season

When you are creating your greenhouse, your plants won't have to depend on the weather. Anybody would be delighted to know that they could grow any herb, fruit, or vegetable they want without having to worry about the weather. Any seed you decide to plant in your greenhouse will take root and grow even though they might not have under the best circumstances when grown outside.

The best advantage of having your greenhouse is you can use various techniques to keep it at a constant temperature. By doing this, you will cause less stress on your plants. Plus, you will have more growth early in the growing season. One technique is known as thermal solar mass. To use this method, you will use natural materials that can absorb, store, and release thermal heat. You could also buy and use heating fans or other heaters.

CHAPTER 6:

Temperature and Humidity for a Greenhouse

A irflow is very important for healthy plant growth in a greenhouse, particularly in the heat of summer as temperatures (hopefully) soar. The air needs to keep moving which will prevent heat from building up and damaging your plants.

Most greenhouses will come with vents and/or windows to help with the movement of air. A good quality greenhouse will have louver vents at ground level which draw in cold air (which is heavier than hot air) and then vents at the top which allows hot air to rise out of the greenhouse. This creates a very natural movement of air which your plants appreciate.

You are looking for a greenhouse with windows and vents that account for around a third of the entire roof area. They do not all need to be at roof level and, ideally, you will want vents at different levels.

If your greenhouse isn't suitably ventilated, then you are going to encourage all sorts of diseases such as fungal problems, powdery mildew, and botrytis. Worse still a greenhouse that is too hot will end up killing some of your plants.

You can leave the door open in the summer, but this can be a security problem depending on where your greenhouse is located.

The other disadvantage of leaving a door open is that pets, particularly cats, will decide to investigate your greenhouse. Dogs, cats, and chickens will cause havoc in your greenhouse from eating plants and fruits to sitting on plants. If you do have pets and want to leave the door open, then a wire panel will keep out most animals except cats.

Window or door screens can be used to keep out unwanted visitors, but the downside of these is that they can also keep out vital pollinating insects!

Mice and other rodents can find their way into your greenhouse through open windows or doors so it can be worth installing an ultrasonic device to keep them out. Of course, cats are excellent rodent deterrents but cause their unique brand of chaos!

Shade Cloth and Paint

This is one of the simplest ways for you to provide shade for your plants.

Shade paint is applied to the outside of your glass, and it diffuses the sun and keeps some of the heat out. Modern shade paints are very clever and will react to the sunlight. When it is raining then the shade paint remains clear, but as the sun comes out, the paint turns white, reflects the sunlight.

Shade fabric is another way to cool your greenhouse, and this is put on the outside of your greenhouse to prevent the sunlight from getting to your plants. It is best installed on the outside of your greenhouse, but you can put it inside, though it will not be as effective. When it is outside, it stops the sun's rays from penetrating your greenhouse but when on the inside the sunlight is already in the greenhouse and generating heat.

Shading alone though is not going to protect your plants from heat damage. Combine this with good ventilation and humidity control to provide your plants with the best possible growing environment.

Shade cloth is a lightweight polyethylene knitted fabric available in densities from 30% to 90% to keep out less or more of the sun's rays. It is not only suitable for greenhouses but is used in cold frames and other applications. It is mildew and rot resistant, water permeable, and does not become brittle over time.

It provides great ventilation and diffuses the light, keeping your greenhouse cooler. It can help reduce the need to run fans in the summer and is quick to install and remove.

A reflective shade is good because instead of absorbing the sun's rays it reflects them. This is better if you can get hold of it because it will be more efficient at keeping the greenhouse cool. The reflective shade cloth is more expensive than a normal shade cloth, but it is worth the money for the additional benefits.

For most applications, you will want a shade cloth that is 50–60% density, but in hotter climates or with light-sensitive plants higher densities such as 70–80% will be necessary. A lot of people use higher-density shade cloth on the roof and lower-density cloth on the walls.

Shade cloth is typically sold by the foot or meter, depending on where you are located, though you can find it sold in pre-made sizes. These are usually hemmed and include grommets for attaching the cloth to the greenhouse.

Shade cloth with a density of 70% allows 30% of light to pass through it. For most vegetables, in the majority of climates, a shade cloth of 30–50% will be sufficient. If you are shading people, then you will want to go up to a density of 80–90%.

Air Flow

Keeping the air moving in your greenhouse during summer can be difficult, particularly in larger greenhouses. Many of the larger electrical greenhouse heaters will double up as air blowers in the summer just by using the fan without the heating element been turned on.

However, using a fan is down to whether or not you have electricity in your greenhouse, which not all of us will have. Although you can use solar energy to run your fan, you will find that it is hard to generate enough energy to keep it going all day.

Automatic Vents

These are an absolute godsend for any gardener and will help keep your plants alive and stop you from having to get up early to open vents!

Automatic vents will open the windows as the temperature rises. This is usually by a cylinder of wax which expands in the heat, opening the window, and then contracts as the temperature cools which closes the window. These do have a finite lifetime, typically lasting a few years but are easily replaced.

One technique that can help keep your greenhouse cool is to damp down the paths and the floor. As the water evaporates, it will help keep the greenhouse cool.

Choosing an Exhaust Fan

For larger greenhouses, you will want an exhaust fan. This is overkill for a smaller greenhouse, but anyone choosing a larger structure will benefit from installing one.

Your exhaust fan needs to be able to change the air in your greenhouse in between 60 and 90 seconds. Fans are rated by cubic feet per minute (CFM), for which you will need to calculate the volume of your greenhouse which is done simply by multiplying the length by the width by the average height.

To measure the average height, measure straight down to the floor from halfway up a roof rafter. It doesn't have to be precise as a few inches either way isn't going to make a significant difference. To determine the cubic feet per minute rating, you need you simply multiply the volume by ¾. Then you will need to find a fan that is near to or greater than this value.

Be careful and double-check your calculations as a fan that is too small will not provide you with enough cooling. Together with a fan, shading cloth or paint, and damping down it will help ensure the greenhouse is kept cool and your plants thrive.

Although your greenhouse may be too small for a fan or you may not have any electricity, at the very least you need windows though louver vents will help a lot. Making sure there is adequate ventilation in your greenhouse is vital so don't skip this step when setting up your greenhouse!

CHAPTER 7:

Greenhouse Irrigation System

One of the main issues you will face with a greenhouse is keeping your plants watered. In hot weather, they can dry out very quickly, and this can cause problems such as leaf, flower, or fruit drop which you want to avoid.

In the hottest weather, and more so in hotter climates, you will need to water your plants two or three times a day to keep them healthy no matter how good your cooling system is!

If you are planning to irrigate your greenhouse, then the need to be sited near to water and/or electricity can heavily influence your choice of location.

There are a lot of different irrigation systems on the market with widely varying prices, so you do need to spend some time considering your requirements before rushing out to buy one.

Some plants require more water than others, so depending on what you are growing you may want to get an automatic irrigation system that can deliver differing quantities of water to different plants.

You also want a system that can grow with you as you put more plants in your greenhouse. At certain times within the season, you will have more plants in your greenhouse than at others, so your irrigation system needs to be able to support this extra demand.

You do need to be careful because any irrigation system that is introducing too much water to your greenhouse could end up making it too damp, which will encourage the growth of diseases. This is one reason why you need to have your drainage and ventilation right to prevent damage to your greenhouse ecosystem.

You typically have two choices about how to deliver water to your plants, either through spray heads or a drip system. The former will spray water over everything in your greenhouse. The downside of this is that it can encourage powdery mildew on certain plants, but the spray can help damp down your greenhouse. It can also be a bit hit and miss as to how much ends up in the soil of your plants. If you are growing in containers, then a spray system may not deliver water precisely enough.

Drip systems though will deliver water precisely to containers and give each container exactly the right amount of water, so no plant goes thirsty!

The downside of most irrigation systems is that they require electricity, which can be difficult, expensive, or even impossible for some greenhouse owners to install. You can purchase solar-powered irrigation systems which will do the job, but they can struggle on duller days.

The water will come into the greenhouse with piping and correctly locating this is important. Hanging it from the ceiling and running it along the walls helps keep it out of the way and stops it from getting damaged. Running the piping along the floor is a recipe for disaster as you are bound to end up putting a container on it and damaging it!

You will need a water supply and ideally mains water, but you can run some irrigation systems from water butts. You will have to check regularly that the water butt has enough water in it, but it is still much easier than manually watering your plants!

Overhead Misters

If you grow mostly or all one type of plant, then an overhead watering method is a great choice because you can water all your plants evenly and easily. For larger greenhouses, this is a great system because it will water a large area quickly.

The downside of this type of system is that it involves a great waste of water since it ends up everywhere in the greenhouse, not only in the containers where the plants are.

Your plants end up getting a lot of water on their leaves. If they are over-crowded or ventilation is poor, then this can cause problems such as powdery mildew and make your plants more susceptible to disease.

Mat Irrigation

You can buy capillary matting which works as an irrigation system for your plants. This is a special mat that is designed to draw up water which is then absorbed by your plants through moisture wicks that go into the soil of your containers.

The mat is kept moist by a drip watering system, so you do not have to run water piping throughout your greenhouse. It can just go to strategic points where it feeds the capillary matting.

This is a relatively cheap method of irrigation and is very simple to install. The big advantage is it is very efficient in its use of water, and there is little risk of overwatering your plants!

Drip Tubing

This is special tubing that you run throughout your greenhouse. It has tubes attached to it that run to the roots of each container to supply water directly to the soil. The big advantage of most drip systems is that you can control the amount of water that drips on your plants. This means that plants that need more water can get it and plants that need less don't get over-watered.

This is set to drip at a certain rate or to operate on a timer so it waters at regular intervals. It will depend on the type of system you buy as to whether it is constant or timed. Timed is by far the best as it allows greater control of the delivery of water, reducing the risks of over-watering.

This is a very water-efficient method of watering your greenhouse with minimal wastage. It can also be set up to be completely automatic, which reduces the time you spend managing your greenhouse.

With some of the more advanced drip watering systems, you have sensors in the ground that monitor moisture levels and turn on the water when the soil becomes too dry.

If you are growing directly in the soil, then the type of soil will influence your drip rate. Heavy clay soil will take longer to absorb water, so it needs less water than lighter soil because in clay it will puddle and pool, which you want to avoid.

Planning your drip watering system is relatively easy. You need to divide your greenhouse into an equal number of sectors, and each area will hold plants with similar water requirements.

Some irrigation systems will allow you to install a fertilizer injector. This is useful as you can get your irrigation system to automatically feed your plants too! Depending on the system this can be set to deliver liquid fertilizer constantly or at specified intervals. This, though, is typically found in more expensive systems, and you need to be very careful in your choice of liquid feed to prevent clogging up the system.

The key with drip irrigation systems is to apply a little water frequently to maintain the soil moisture levels. This is a very water-efficient system that is easy to expand and works no matter what size plants you are growing.

Most people who own a greenhouse and install an irrigation system will choose a drip watering system. They are easily available and very affordable though, as, with anything, you can spend more money and get more advanced systems.

CHAPTER 8:

Maintenance Problems

Issues can pop up in greenhouses no matter how well you treat your plants. Do you not feel bad if any of these problems pop up? Simply look back at this information and figure out how you can solve the issue quickly and effectively. We are going to go over every common greenhouse problem you may encounter on your gardening journey. We will look into the problem in detail, learn why it occurs, and how to fix it. Let's get started.

First, let's look into what to do if you get bugs in your greenhouse. Is there something that you would think of dealing with outside? Obviously, you do not want to need to deal with them inside of your greenhouse. The first reason is that you are already in a structure—you should not have to deal with something like bugs. The second reason is if bugs are in your greenhouse, it is not like they're merely going to be like when they are outside. If bugs are in your greenhouse, they probably think that they are there to stay. You will need to do something to get them out of your greenhouse. They are not going to fly away like they were outside.

Let's start by looking into why bugs get into greenhouses. If there is any space that allows insects to get into your greenhouse—like a crack or hole or even vent or door that was open for a few seconds—bugs can get in. Bugs go inside greenhouses because they know they're filled with plants and because they want to pollinate them. Bugs can also go to clean houses to explore. Other bugs are looking for plants to eat. You really do not want these latter bugs in your greenhouse. You definitely do not want your plants to get eaten by anyone except for you.

Next, let's look into some ways that you can prevent bugs from getting into your greenhouse. One of the easiest ways to avoid getting bumped into your greenhouses is to look at the things that you bring inside. If you are bringing a plant, make sure there are no bugs in it. If you are bringing in new soil, make sure you do the same. Anything that you bring in should be checked to ensure that there are no bugs that could hurt your plants on them.

Another thing that you can do to avoid getting bugs in your greenhouses to make sure that they do not have a way in. Make sure that all cracks and holes are filled. Also, if you have a fence, you could consider putting a screen on them. You can put screens on the windows as well. You can also make sure that when you come in and out of the greenhouse, you do so quickly, and you do not leave the door open.

It is also a good idea not to plant anything outside around your greenhouse. If you put plants around the outside of your greenhouse, these plants can attract bugs. If you attract insects next to your greenhouse, they will probably know that there are plants inside, and they will probably find a way in. You want to keep all of your outdoor plants far away from the greenhouse to avoid this happening.

Now, let's look into what to do if you already have bugs inside of your greenhouse. In an outdoor garden, you might reach for pesticides. This is not a great idea inside of a greenhouse, not only because they are toxic chemicals, but because in such a small space, they can be a hazard. One helpful way to catch bugs inside of your greenhouse is to use bug traps like tape. You can hang out tape all around in your greenhouse, and it will not affect your plants. However, it will catch the bugs that you do not want to be there. You could also consider making sure to get rid of anything that will attract bugs. For example, make sure that there is no standing water available in your greenhouse. If your bugs are not attracted to anything inside of your greenhouse, they may leave. If you are having a hard time with bugs in your greenhouse, you could always ask a professional exterminator for help.

Something that can be problematic is your greenhouse's diseases. Many things can cause diseases in your plants. These problems can come from mold, bacteria, and viruses. Greenhouse diseases, sometimes, can be hard to beat. Let's look into some ways that you can prevent these diseases from occurring in your greenhouse.

What is the most important thing that you can do to prevent disease in your greenhouses? It is to sanitize. You want to make sure that you sanitize everything after you use it. You will need to sanitize 2, trays, and even shelves. If you do not sanitize your tools, it increases your risk of spreading disease inside of your greenhouse from plant to plant. This is because if one plant had a disease and you used a shovel to scoop it out and throw it away, and then use the same shovel in another plant, the new plant would probably get the disease as well just from being touched with the same shovel. The spread of disease in plants inside greenhouses is similar to the spread of disease in humans. If you stay clean, you will have a much better chance of not spreading diseases.

You allow someone to watch your humidity and make sure that you are greenhouse does not get overly humid. If your greenhouse is too humid, mold and fungus are likely to grow on your soil. If these grow in your soil, your plants will get the disease because of them. Mold and fungus can also spread very quickly and easily. It is something that you want to avoid having in your greenhouse.

When watering your plants, you will want to make sure that the tool does not touch your plant's insurgencies, and you will also want to make sure that the water does not splash while you are watering. If water splashes from one plant to another, it can spread disease. Because of this, you will want to use a tool for watering that does not allow water to splash. You will want to use a tool that has a light spray that soaks into the soil and does not splash at all.

One last thing that you can do to protect your plants from disease is to look at them every day. Walk around your greenhouse and look for signs of disease. Look for things that seem out of the ordinary. If you see a plant that does not look healthy, consider taking it out of the greenhouse and quarantining it for a while. This will allow you to tell if the plant is infected with the disease as well as keep it away from other healthy plants to make sure that they do not catch a disease if it has one. With this process, it is helpful to know what plants look like when they are diseased. If the plant has mold or fungus, you will probably be able to tell right away. If it has mold growing in the soil or mushrooms growing in the ground, it means that it has mold or fungus. This is one of the most natural diseases to tell if your plant has. Another sign that your plant has a disease is that it has large, raised brown lumps on its leaves. These lumps typically mean the plant is sick. Plants that seem to be dying even though you are taking great care of them can be diseased as well.

Diseases in greenhouses are not fun to deal with. You should be able to handle them with success. If you take the necessary precautions to make sure that diseases do not enter your plants, and take it seriously when a plant is looking unhealthy, you should have success in keeping this problem away.

CHAPTER 9:

Pests and Diseases

Did You Know?

Thriving greenhouses are an open invitation for pests and critters. Its warm and humid environment attracts pesky intruders from near and far, making them feel right at home. Plus, who can deny fresh and juicy fruits and veggies ready to be devoured?

Without natural enemies lurking by, greenhouses become the ideal environment for pest infestation and multiplication. Often, the pest situation escalates at a faster pace indoors than outdoors.

The Most Common Pests Found Inside a Greenhouse & How to Control Them

Greenhouse pests can be divided into three categories. These include sap-feeding insects, pollen feeders, and leaf eaters (like caterpillars and slugs). Most pest prevention techniques help deter common insects.

However, some pests are harder to control. It's why your greenhouse plants require constant monitoring and additional protection for successful cultivation.

Let's have a look at the common bugs you might come across during greenhouse gardening:

Sap-Feeding Insects

Sap-feeding insects have special sucking (and piercing) mouthparts. They use it to feed on plant cells (like mesophyll) and sap. Some common sap-feeding insects found inside the greenhouses include aphids, mites, mealybugs, scale insects, and whiteflies.

Plant Damage

Sap-feeding insects drain the liquid part of plants along with the nutrients and minerals it transports. In turn, this strips the essential nutrients required for plant growth. It also causes plants to become severely dehydrated.

They are known as one of the most destructive greenhouse gardening pests.

That is because pest damage from these insects is often undetectable during the initial phases of the infestation. Eventually, you might notice a shiny, translucent look in the affected plants. They will also feel sticky.

Without intervention, the sticky plants may develop a black, sooty appearance. It marks the arrival of a fungus (called sooty mold) that grows on honeydew (i.e., sugary droppings) excreted by sap-feeding insects. The sweet droppings might attract ants too.

Other signs include:

- Leaf stippling (i.e., spotted appearance)
- Yellow leaves and discoloration
- Leaf curling (i.e., distorted leaves, with edges curled inwards)
- Galls (i.e., plant tissues look swollen due to abnormal outgrowths)

Aphids

Aphids (often called plant lice) are small, slow-moving insects. Greenhouse infestation begins when one or two-winged insects come inside through an open vent or door. Their high reproductive cycle and resistance to most insecticides make aphids a threat to greenhouse plants.

Aphids are known to form clusters of colonies on sap-containing parts of host plants (i.e., leaves and stems). These insects extract plant sap by piercing into the target area and using their beak-like mouths to suck.

They typically attack the young leaves of most food crops, fruit trees, and flowering plants except for garlic and chives. Aphids feed on the tenderest part of the host plant, usually found under the leaf. Their presence attracts ants and encourages mold infestations due to their sugary droppings. Besides this, aphids can transmit plant diseases.

Pest Control

Most gardeners recommend running multiple insecticide applications to manage aphid invasion. We recommend 2–3 applications conducted between 3–7 day gaps. You can alter the schedule depending on the severity of the situation.

Additionally, using alternate insecticides for each cycle can delay resistance against specific formulas. In turn, this maximizes the chances of achieving desirable results. You can also use neem oil and diatomaceous earth to control aphid infestation.

Mites

Mites (or spider mites) have a distinctive dusty-like appearance. These microscopic arachnids are distant cousins of ticks and spiders. They reside in the leaves' underside, like most sap-sucking pests, of ornamental plants, shrubs, and fruits.

Like aphids, they reproduce rapidly, causing severe crop damage.

Spider mites pierce the cell wall to suck sap and succulent plant tissues. In turn, this causes spots as most of the nutrients inside the host plant get drained. After a while, nutrient deficiency leads to yellow spots. These patches might appear throughout the affected leaf/stem. Without intervention, these plants might die.

Other noticeable signs of these tiny pests include curled leaves, deformed leaves, and a trail of fine web-like silk strands.

Pest Control

Pesticide resistance makes them difficult to control mites. They are also challenging to eliminate due to their hidden locations and microscopic size. These factors make repeated insecticide application necessary to destroy mite eggs and the population.

Gardeners recommend spraying pesticides on the lower and upper sides of the affected leaves. Two to three applications scheduled between five-day gaps generally improve effectiveness. Introducing natural predators like ladybugs and lacewings also helps.

Whiteflies

Whiteflies resemble small moths, but they look like moths that are dusted with white powder. They are not actual flies but tiny sap-sucking insects with wings. Adult whiteflies only flutter away if their breeding and feeding grounds are disturbed.

Otherwise, they prefer to stay under leaves to suck the succulent stems and sap continuously.

They mainly attack ornamental flowering plants such as hibiscus, gerbera daisy, poinsettia, and geranium. Besides this, they are found in vegetable patches. Usual feeding sites include tomatoes, eggplants, and cucumbers.

Like all other sap-suckers, whiteflies consume plant juices by piercing into sap-filled cells. Common signs of whiteflies include discolored leaves, sooty mold, honeydew droppings, and wilting. Severe infestations might lead to crop reduction and plant death.

Pest Control

Whitefly removal revolves around biological and chemical control. Garlic sprays, neem oil, insecticidal soaps, and sticky traps placed on fruit trees are commonly used for pest control. Applications are spaced out between 2–5 days, depending on the severity of the infestation.

Pesticide resistance can be a concern. It is strongly advised to switch between insecticides to improve efficiency.

Apart from this, you can introduce beneficial insects and natural predators to greenhouses. Standard choices include whitefly parasites, lacewings, ladybugs, dragonflies, and hummingbirds. Most of these predators work well during the initial infestation stage as they feed on whitefly eggs and immature larva.

Nevertheless, their presence does deter reproduction rates. In turn, this facilitates other pest control methods.

Pollen Feeders: Thrips, Shore Flies, and Fungus Gnats

Pollen-feeding insects are small, often winged creatures. This category includes thrips, shore flies, fungus gnats, and small flies. These insects hover around flowers, often consuming nectar and helping with plant pollination. These insects leave traces of black feces and discarded exoskeletons wherever they go.

Plant Damage

Adult insects are nothing but a nuisance, but their larvae can be dangerous for plant growth. The immature pests feed on overwatered roots and inhibit nutrient intake.

Common signs of infestation include:

- Yellow speckled leaves or silvered appearance
- Spotted flower petals
- Distorted fruits
- Visible black spots/droppings
- Some spotting on flowers
- Wilted leaves
- Scarred roots

- Reduced yield

Moreover, you will notice a swarm of mosquito-like insects flying over infected plants and larvae present at the back of infested leaves.

Pest control for pollen feeders works in the same way as sap-sucking insects.

Slugs and Caterpillars

Caterpillars and slugs might make an occasional appearance inside the greenhouse. They are categorized as defoliators (i.e., leaf eaters). They feed on young, succulent plants with tender leaves and juicy sap of seedlings, vegetables, flowers, and more. The most distinctive sign of these notorious pests is half-chewed leaves and bite marks.

Unlike other pests, they are visible to the naked eye. Their sluggish movement makes them detectable and easier to catch compared to other problems.

Plant Damage

These pests often attack plants at night, leaving trails of slime in the affected areas. Use a flashlight to check the underside of leaves when you search for them.

Other signs include:

- Big, ragged holes on leaves, vegetables, bulbs, flowers, and other parts of your greenhouse plants
- Leaves with bite marks
- No leaves on seedlings

Overall, their presence leads to damaged crops and reduced yield.

Pest Control

Their size and slow movement make pest control relatively easier if the infestation gets detected early. All you have to do is pick and toss these pesky pests into a bucket filled with soapy water. You can also use some insecticidal soap/spray to kill them off.

You can also use homemade pest repellants on them or neem oil to eliminate potential threats. Make sure that leaves are thoroughly washed to remove eggs and larvae.

What's More?

If you live in the countryside or open area, expect bigger pests to move into your greenhouse. Mice, squirrels, snakes, and raccoons might sneak in through open vents. You may notice they're through sounds, half-eaten fruits, a trail of footprints, and feces.

Besides setting some animal traps, there is not much an average gardener can do to remove these pests from the site.

Therefore, we suggest calling an exterminator or another professional for help. Most experts will figure out a way to lure the pest out without compromising on plant health.

3 Common Greenhouse Plant Diseases

There are three types of major plant diseases that you might experience during greenhouse gardening. These include fungal infections, viruses, and bacterial diseases.

Fungal Infection

Fungal infections such as powdery mildew, root rot, and phytophthora might spread inside the greenhouse. High humidity and high moisture levels are often the leading cause of fungal growth. That's why; you must control moisture levels on leaves and stems. Also, do not overwater your plant. They might get waterlogged. Visible signs of fungal growth include:

- Wilting
- Fuzzy lumps on leaves and stems
- Collapsed roots
- Yellowish tinge or complete discoloration

Most fungal infections target surface areas like leaves and stems. They are easy to cure. Neem oil and disinfectants are preferable choices for fungal removal. In severe cases, discard the affected area or uproot the infected plant to minimize spreading.

Bacterial Disease

There are four common categories of bacterial diseases (i.e., wilt, soft rot, necrosis, and tumors). They are grouped according to the severity of plant damage and symptoms. Blight, canker, crown gall, citrus canker, and blackleg are some known bacterial infections.

The common signs of bacterial infection in plants include:

- Spotted leaf
- Rotten fruits and vegetation
- Wilting
- Galls and overgrowths
- Cankers and scabs, indicating erosion
- Specks and blights
- Distorted steams and leaves

In short, your plants will look sticky and gummy when they get sick. It's advised to quarantine them or remove them right away. Some gardeners suggest uprooting them and destroying them quickly before the disease spreads to neighboring crops.

Virus

Several plant-related viruses can destroy greenhouse crops and inhibit growth. They are either air-borne, water-borne, or through vectors.

Common virus carriers include aphids and thrips. Most viruses attack specific species or plant. You should monitor susceptible plants closely to detect signs of infection.

CHAPTER 10:

Seed Starting

The method of propagation in plant cultivation can either be sexual or asexual. Sexual propagation involves the production of a new plant using seeds while asexual propagation is the creation of a new plant using the leaves, buds, or roots of a parent plant. If you do not have the patience to seed start your greenhouse, you can always propagate asexually as it is a faster process than seed propagation. But basically, it is more rewarding to cultivate plants from seed in a greenhouse. When seed starting, it is important to ensure suitable environmental conditions that will aid the germination of the seed. Firstly, fresh and quality seeds should be used because they are usually insect-free and disease-resistant. If possible, use hybrid seeds as they produce sturdy and vigorous plants that give higher yields. In a situation where seeds from the preceding growing season are to be used, the seeds should be sterilized and tested before they are used. The perfect condition for seed germination is the right amount of water, temperature, light, and oxygen. Seeds are grown in greenhouses usually do not have a dormancy period as long as the environmental condition created is favorable. However, the seeds of some plants do not germinate easily because of their hard protective outer cover called the seed coat. These seeds can be softened by scrapping or better still, soaking them into sulfuric acid to increase their water absorption rate. Seed germination starts as soon as the seeds can absorb water from the potting soil (growing medium).

Growing Medium

The following can be used as potting soil in the greenhouse; coarse sand, garden soil, perlite, compost, peat moss, coir fiber, vermiculite, or in some cases, a combination of two or more. Each of these potting soils come with their individual properties and advantages such as the rate of soil aeration, moisture retention, adequate drainage, etc. This is why the chosen growing medium should first be tested and the pH determined before seed planting. A pH range between 5.5–6.5 is advisable for optimum seed growth. The soluble salt in the medium should be maintained low enough and there should be adequate moisture and air space in the growing medium as well. The temperature and moisture levels are usually determined by the type of plant to be cultivated. The need for adequate moisture content in the medium is to reduce the shrinking of the medium. You should also avoid using a compacted growing medium because of poor aeration.

Container

The type of containers used in greenhouses includes plug trays and wooden flats. The traditional wooden flats are rarely used by growers although they are good for propagating large root plants. Nutrients are readily made available to the plants using this container but the con side of it is that the spacing in the traditional wooden flats does not allow for the complete utilization of the greenhouse space. And it can also be a bit labor-intensive and costly because the much-growing medium is consumed when this container is used. The plug trays are generally a common type of container used. They come in different sizes and shapes. Before seed planting, you should decide if the seed will germinate and fully grow in the same container or will be later transferred to another container for finishing. This will determine the size of the container to choose from. It is important to choose the right size of the container according to the expected root size of the plant and also sterilize the container before using it. If you are using bleach for sterilization, the ratio of the bleach mixture should be 1:10, that is, 1 portion of bleach to 10 portions of water. The container should be deep enough to contain the root size and big enough to avoid crowded seedlings. By using plug trays, the growing space in the greenhouse is completely utilized and the small size of the cells consumes only a little growing medium and therefore production cost is reduced compared to the traditional wooden flats. You should keep in mind however that, the small growing medium consumed when plug trays are used simply means limiting nutrients is available to the plants and therefore will require more fertilization and also more irrigation supply than the wooden flats would require. Above all, choose a container that suits the plant you intend to cultivate and ensure that the container has good drainage.

Seed Planting

When the right container and the suitable growing medium are made ready, the seed can then be planted. It is advisable to use seed raising mix for good seed germination. You should also ensure to avoid compacting the soil medium and after planting your seed, use a misting system to water the medium. Many growers automate the watering system to make it less labor-intensive. Seeds that need light to germinate are best planted shallow while the ones that do not need light to germinate can be planted deep into the medium. To ensure the rapid and uniform germination of the seed, the right temperature range must be ensured.

Once the seed starts germinating, attention should be given to aeration in the medium to ensure that the plant respires well.

Fertilization

While it is true that adding fertilizers to plants aid their rapid growth, too much application will eventually cause damage to the plants. It should be noted that most growing medium already contains nutrients and the addition of more fertilizer will affect the pH of the medium. Situations that demand fertilizer application are when plants start showing signs of stress as a result of lack of nutrients, when the plants' growth is slow and needs to be hastened, and also when the growing medium is nutrient-deficient and its biological activity needs to be enhanced.

In order to keep the seed growth healthy, it is important to pay attention to the pH of the medium and add fertilizer slowly and gradually. There are different types of fertilizers and each one affects plant growth differently. Fertilizers that contain high nitrate (but not excess) and low phosphorus are advisable as they enhance uniform growth, sturdy root, and a high pH in the medium.

The soluble salt content in the medium should, however, be kept low to prevent root rot diseases. It is also a maintenance practice to rinse off plants after fertilizer application on a sunny day.

Irrigation System

The irrigation system set up in greenhouse gardening is usually different from the irrigation set up for open field gardening. Moisture content is generally not applied in large volumes in greenhouses. Irrigation in greenhouses is applied manually or through overhead delivery which can be an automated delivery system or semi-automated delivery. In manual delivery systems, the cost is reduced but the downside of using this system is the risk of non-uniform plant growth as a result of uneven watering. And you may also find that manual delivery is a bit labor-intensive except you are an experienced irrigator who takes irrigation as a hobby. The sprinkler system for overhead delivery can either be automatic or semi-automatic as stated earlier, and there is a more evenly distributed watering in the greenhouse when overhead irrigation is used. To set up an automated overhead delivery system can be expensive because of the sensors and other tools used to sense the environmental condition and the requirement of the growing plant and respond accordingly. If you have enough capital to install a completely automated overhead system, do not hesitate as it improves your chances of producing quality yield faster and hence get a better ROI (return on investment). In a semi-automatic overhead delivery system, it is the responsibility of the grower to determine when the seeds need watering and then schedule the time to go on and off accordingly. However, you should ensure that the sprinkler system is well designed such that it supplies an even distribution in the greenhouse. For the majority of the germinated seed, the medium is allowed to dry at least halfway before replenishing the lost moisture in a small quantity. If the irrigation system is scheduled, it should be done in such a way that it does not leave too much water in the growing medium, and the container used should be the type that allows easy drainage.

To successfully propagate your plant from seed, seeds generally require moisture to enhance their germination but you should avoid growing them in a waterlogged soil medium and remember to prune the seedlings as they grow. Except for plants that take very long to germinate, it is always best to grow your plants from seed. And while you do that, you should ensure to supply the seeds with their required growing environment because different seeds require different growing conditions.

CHAPTER 11:

Greenhouse Equipment

Having the best greenhouse equipment is crucial for efficiently managing your greenhouse. The equipment will help in your operation, maintenance, and improvement of the greenhouse, and there is a wide variety of equipment and other accessories for your entire greenhouse in the market.

The choice of equipment to use depends on the types of crops and the climatic conditions of the area. That is, are you located in an area that experiences heavy snow and a lot of wind, or are you in an area that experiences extreme heat or cold? This information is important when buying greenhouse equipment.

The equipment used only for raising seedlings will be different from those you would use for full-cycle planting fruits or vegetables. Your choice of equipment and other accessories will ensure your ability to produce high-quality crops and maintain active produce for all-year-round crops. You should keep the greenhouse structure warm and properly managed to create more space for plant germination.

Depending on the type of crop, planting can be on the floor or the benches. A fixed peninsula and movable benches are highly recommended, as they help in creating more growing space. Other equipment like overhead conveyor trolleys and carts can contribute to reducing the cost of material handling.

Basic Equipment

When you think of starting your greenhouse garden, there are basic considerations you need to think about, such as where to get the seeds, pots, and trays to plant your crops.

The choice of these greenhouse containers will have an impact on how the vegetables, herbs, and fruits grow.

The containers you use in the garden should be able to grip the soil and promote good health to the seeds. They should also offer enough room for the roots to grow and provide an excellent drainage system. This ensures the crops are in good condition and promote their growth.

Containers can hold several planting trays and pots to provide crop growth and stability, and as a result, there will be upward growth of the crops. These containers can be in the form of plugs, flats, pots, and hanging baskets. A larger container can fit several pots inside and provide enough space to grow the seeds.

Hanging baskets are great for planting your vegetables and herbs in the garden. There are plenty of these baskets in the market, and they will provide enough space for your crops' growth. Most of the baskets will be plastic or coconut fiber, while others will be made of ceramic metal. You can buy any material based on your budget.

You would use flats and plugs during the germination stage. They ensure the vegetables grow separately and keep your garden neat. Most gardeners prefer pots made of clay, as they give the growing of plants like fruits, flowers, and vegetables a more traditional look. If you're on a budget, you can buy plastic pots or wood pots, which are more durable and cheaper. You can dispose of plastic and wood pots much easier than clay pots.

You can also consider the use of seedboxes to help you in the germination of the seeds. The boxes can be made of plastic or wood material and they provide you with excellent space to grow your fruits and vegetables.

How to Choose Good Containers and Pots

If you're using porous containers, you will find that you have to continue watering the crops, as the soil dries out very quickly. This can lead to wasting water and increase the cost of water. In non-porous containers, you use less water because the soil grips moisture, thus, retaining enough water content for a day.

Mobility of the pots and containers is also important, especially if plan to have all-year-round crops in the garden. They should be made of lightweight material to make it easy to move them around.

Choosing the right container will contribute significantly to the growth of vegetables, herbs, and fruits in your greenhouse.

Furniture to Store Greenhouse Equipment

Shelves: You need furniture that will help you arrange all the containers and provide adequate shelving in the greenhouse. If you have a small space in the greenhouse, you can use shelves to boost the growing space.

There are movable greenhouse shelves that you can move out and back inside during favorable climatic conditions.

Always remember that double shelving can affect the amount of lighting required by the crops.

You can build temporary shelves or have permanent shelves attached to the structure to start your seedlings. You can also have shelves built beneath the garden benches to help you create more space in the greenhouse.

You can build shelves made of wood, glass, or metal. The wire mesh you use in building the shelves helps in draining the excess water from the crops.

Another important reason for creating shelves is to ensure all the crops are separate from one another to avoid cross-pollination. Depending on the size of the shelves, it can store more pots and containers.

Garden benches: Furniture inside the greenhouse are garden benches. The greenhouse structure determines the size of the benches in the garden, and these benches can be temporary or permanently built. Installing benches is great for optimizing the growing space in the garden, and benches are ideal for regular movement and creating new plant arrangements.

Planters: These are widely common in today's modern greenhouse gardens. Long and deep planters are highly recommended for growing fruits, vegetables, or any other food crops. The planters are designed in such a way that each can only hold a single vegetable or fruit plant.

Lighting System Equipment

The amount of light inside the greenhouse determines the level of sunlight in the greenhouse. If the amount of sunlight in the greenhouse is not strong enough, you can supplement it with artificial light.

Before choosing the lighting system to use for boosting plant growth, you need to determine the amount of solar radiation available in that area, as that will affect the amount of light needed for photosynthesis.

Other factors you need to look at are the size and type of greenhouse structure. You also need to consider the crops growing, as some of them require high-intensity light, while others will do better in low light or shade.

You should consider the space available for hanging the lighting system, and it should be easy to adjust based on the crops' needs. For example, as some plants, like fruits, increase in height as they grow, the lighting system should be moved upwards. Therefore, you need to factor in the wiring system and the socket space.

Some of the tools for providing artificial light include:

- **Light intensity meter:** This instrument has an installed universal-sensor probe that measures the intensity of light at any angle. The equipment monitor can maintain an ideal growing light for all plants in the garden.
- **Grow lights:** Grow lights are excellent for providing a cool and warm light for the growth of house plants, herbs, and fruits. The grow lights act as a replacement for sunlight when growing plants indoors. There are different types of grow lights in the market to choose from, such as fluorescent, LEDs, high-pressure sodium, among others.

- **Seedling lights:** As the seeds germinate, they require a lot of light; therefore, you need to place them in an area where they can have maximum access to light. Each plant grown requires a different light intensity, and most plants in a greenhouse garden require a high light intensity to flourish. You can have fluorescent bulbs installed in the garden to provide maximum light to all your crops.

- **High-intensity discharge lamp (HID):** If you have a large greenhouse structure with big plants like fruits and flowers, you need to install HID lamps. These lamps emit more light compared to other types of lights, boosting plant growth. The lamp fixtures have reflectors fitted on them to reflect the light back to the crops.

  This type of lamp produces a lot of heat, so you should keep it far away from the plants to avoid burning their leaves.

- **LED lights:** LED lights are suitable for vegetables and herbs, they're the best greenhouse lights and the most efficient for quick plant growth. The lights are long-lasting and easy to install.

Temperature Control and Heating System Equipment

To control the temperature, you need to install an electronic controller in the garden. This control will monitor and manage the temperatures of the heating system and ventilation equipment.

Thermostats: If you have a small greenhouse garden, you can use thermostats that record accurate temperatures within the garden, and they automatically control the temperature in a specific area. Make sure it is installed based on the plant height as this will make it easy to capture accurate readings on temperature conditions.

Thermometer: A thermometer measures the maximum and minimum temperature inside the garden and monitors any temperature changes. It helps in maintaining perfect temperatures for the growth of plants.

When buying a thermometer for the greenhouse, look for one that is reset by a magnet. Although there are other types, the one with a magnet is highly recommended for greenhouses.

Hot air furnace or unit heaters: The unit heater is suitable when the greenhouse is shut down during the winter season to drain the water system. Installing unit heaters is one of the best decisions you can make for your crop production, as they control the temperature inside the greenhouse.

There are different types of heaters and based on your garden needs, such as gas, electric, or propane. You can also choose to use vented on non-vented heaters.

- **EPDM tubing:** Temperature control on the benches or floor is also important. You can place the EPDM tubing on the concrete floor or in a sand layer to provide floor heating. If you plant your crops on the benches, you can place the EPDM tubing on the bench or use a low output radiation pin, which you would place under the bench to keep the area warm.

- **Hot water boiler:** A hot water boiler is the best for maintaining the heating system. Make sure the water temperatures don't go beyond 75°F (24°C). The root zone heat provides uniform temperatures of 70–75°F (21–24°C), which is essential for all plant growth. Root zone heat provides 25% of the heat needed for the coldest nights, while the remaining 75% heat comes from heat exchangers or a radiation pin installed under the gutters or around the perimeter of the greenhouse.

- **Humidistat:** A humidistat equipment is needed to control moisture or humidity within the greenhouse.

In a large-scale operation, you can easily integrate computer controls in the ventilation, lighting, and heating systems. Using computer-controlled systems ensures automatic control of environmental conditions within the greenhouse.

Ventilation Equipment

A proper ventilation system contributes to the growth of your plants. Sunlight changes throughout the year can cause temperature changes in the garden, so you need to have a good venting system installed to control the temperatures.

- **Vents:** You can install vents on the roof or the sides of the structure. Rooftop vents are the most common and one of the best venting systems.
  If you're not around throughout the day, an automatic venting system will be ideal for you.
- **Exhaust fans:** You would use exhaust fans to whisk away excess air and ensure there is a constant supply of fresh air inside.

CHAPTER 12:

Making a Business of Your Greenhouse

I f you have a successful greenhouse that grows beautiful plants and flowers, why not consider making some money from your hobby? You might not have ever thought about your hobby as a profitable business, but if you have at least a little bit of extra time and patience, you can make quite a nice income from your greenhouse.

Find Your Niche

For any grower to be successful, they need to be aware of and be able to make use of current niches and trends in the growing market. The advantage of greenhouse growing is that you can have an extended season of growth that other more natural growers would not have. This means that you can grow special flowers, fruits, and veggies that would not normally be available to others much later in the year.

There is always a market for certain crops, especially when they begin to become out of season, so this creates an immediate cash crop for you to make money.

Special fall flowers such as Dwarf Snapdragons are much sought after by late fall, and typically only greenhouse growers can meet the demand that most retailers need. But along with extending the growing time for rare flowers and produce, in finding your niche, you need to find out what kind of production makes the most money.

Often enough, there are best sellers in the market, such as tomatoes and jalapeno peppers, and the popular demand may vary based upon your geographical area. As soon as you find your niche, you can begin to make a whole lot of money in the process.

Becoming a Business

One of the first things you should do before you start conducting business is to become a business. This means getting a business name, typically done through your county clerk's office. Most who start a small business use a Doing Business as or Assumed Name; this means that income from your business is the same as income from any other place. You add up your income and subtract your expenses and report the final amount on your tax return at the end of the year.

Unless you plan on opening a retail flower store, you probably don't need to collect taxes from your customers as you would be considered a wholesaler. However, if your business grows and you're concerned about your need to collect taxes, you can probably quickly speak to a CPA over the phone and ask. Usually, applying for a tax ID is very easy and probably done at your county clerk's office as well.

These certificates—your Assumed Name and tax ID—are typically very affordable, usually less than twenty dollars each. Don't hesitate to call your county clerk's office first if you want to be sure your chosen business name isn't already taken or aren't sure which certificate is right for you. You can probably also check online as many counties have their website where you can run off the forms you need and can find out the charge.

Once you have your business certificates, you can open a commercial checking account at just about any bank and may also want to check to see if you can reserve a website name that is at least close to your business name.

Important: When coming up with a business name, you can, of course, have it a bit whimsical; people often assume a greenhouse or flower shop has a bit of whimsy or creativity. Just make sure that it still sounds professional and is easy to remember and spell so that potential customers can remember it and find it again very easily. For instance, you might want to avoid "Debbie's Total Supply of Flowers and Plants from Her

Own Greenhouse to Your Table" since it's incredibly long and wordy, but "Deb's Greenhouse and Flower Supply" is much easier to remember!

Finding Customers

So, how to find customers, and what type of items should you sell? Here are some things you want to consider.

First, make sure your gardening is reliable and that you can grow enough of an inventory regularly so that your customers won't be disappointed. Being able to produce one flowering lily plant is all well and good, but if you want actually to make money from your business, you're going to need to produce beautiful flowers regularly.

This will, of course, mean being very attentive to your greenhouse and your plants. No one wants to buy their flowers from someone who comes through with deliveries only when they can. Yes, you'll lose some flowers here and there and, of course, can't always count on how many flowers you can grow, but to be successful with your business, you're going to need to have a pretty reliable idea of what you can and cannot deliver.

Next, you'll need to consider what type of customers you can support with your inventory. Flower shops sometimes have their own greenhouse for their supply, and supermarkets may have a floral shop, but because of how many flowers they need, they may want to deal only with a large commercial greenhouse facility. However, there are many other possibilities when it comes to customers that you can support. For example:

- Do you have any mini markets or corner stores near your home that sell a small number of flowers? Even if you don't see them selling flowers now if you were to talk to the manager or owner of the store, you might be able to convince them to carry a small inventory.

- Restaurants sometimes want fresh flowers for their tables. You may be able to speak to a manager about providing carnations or other colorful blooms for their dining area or décor.

- Retirement communities also sometimes have fresh flowers on their dining tables; you may be able to provide these for them regularly.

- Businesses often give flowers to their employees on secretary's day or when someone has had a baby or other occasion. If you're priced cheaper than large, national florists, you may be able to provide for local businesses when the occasion calls for it.

- Weddings, of course, are big business for many florists. While you may not be ready to supply to very large weddings at a moment's notice, if you spread the word among your friends and relatives, you might find that someone you know is interested in working with you, especially if your costs are lower than national florists.

Many brides today are looking to save money in any way they can, so they may be happy to simply choose from the flowers you have available.

- Your friends and family too may want to see what flowers you have available on special days and occasions. They may check with you for anniversaries, birthdays, and holidays.

Very often, getting the word out there among your friends and family and local businesses is all that's needed to get your first order, which in turn can lead to so many other orders down the road!

Some Important Considerations

Before you just run out and start talking to those retirement home managers and restaurant owners, consider some of the following points:

- **Consider getting a website even if you don't plan on selling online.** A website is a great marketing tool because potential customers will often bookmark your site and visit again when they're ready to purchase. A website address is often easier to remember than a phone number, so customers might visit your site looking for your actual contact information. Websites are usually very affordable if you just need a few pages with your contact info and a few photos of your product.

- **Most places that purchase flowers from you may expect some type of special packaging.** For example, that corner market might be interested in purchasing single blooms that they keep by the cash register for one-at-a-time purchases. However, these blooms are usually wrapped in cellophane and may have new ferns or baby's breath inside. Be prepared with these extra materials and for the wrapping involved; don't just show up with an armful of single blossoms.

- **Stores may also expect you to provide the large vase that these flowers are kept in near the register.** View this as a marketing opportunity; put a card with your business name and phone number or website address on the front of it.

- **Get to know the accessories you need for many of your products.** If you're going to provide bridal bouquets, you'll need the little handles they fit into. Boutonnieres for groomsmen usually are attached with a pin. That retirement community may also ask you to provide vases. Shop for wholesale items online so you can purchase these things very cheaply.

- **If you're very dedicated to making this greenhouse into a successful business, take a flower arranging class.** Putting together bouquets and arrangements is usually part art but part science. Sometimes certain colors or sizes of flowers are just too busy or may look overdone when used together. At the very least, study bouquets you see online and practice some on your own before trying to sell them to a customer.

Another thing you might want to consider about getting customers and selling is to have some marketing material available. At the very least, you should have professional business cards made up so that when you call upon potential customers, you have something you can leave with them, so they have your contact info handy.

You might also be able to make up a flyer or brochure with some featured products. If you can't do this on your own, you can easily hire someone with a marketing degree to do this for you; chances are you might even have a friend with some talent that can easily design some business cards or marketing material. Any nearby office supply center can probably print these things out for a very affordable price.

Calculate Your Profit Window

To be successful with your greenhouse, you need to assess just how profitable the enterprise will be. This means that you need to calculate your potential profit window in advance. First, you need to take into consideration how much money you will have to put into the greenhouse project. If it is just a small amount of money, you can set aside the small amount you may need; if it is a larger amount, you can then plan for that also.

Once this has been established, you can then think about the types of plants you will be growing and approximately how much their valued worth on the market will be. After that, it's just a matter of basic calculation to find out how much profit you would be able to make at the end of the process. Keep close track of your expenses and earnings along the way so that you can make the best use of your produce.

CHAPTER 13:

Plants for Hydroponic Gardening

With hydroponic gardening, you can grow almost anything from houseplants and flowering plants to vegetables and fruits. Whether you are growing them for decoration, health purposes, or seasoning, you will find hydroponic gardening quite beneficial. You can grow your plants in any season and weather and have your supply of fresh herbs, fruits, and vegetables.

Here is a list of the plants that will grow well in various hydroponic systems. Also included some interesting information about each of them.

Herbs

You will be happy to know that many herbs grow exceedingly well in hydroponic systems. Some of them include basil, anise, chamomile, chives, catnip, cilantro, chervil, dill, fennel, mint, lavender, oregano, marjoram, parsley, sage, rosemary, thyme, and tarragon.

- **Basil**: Basil is often grown in a protected environment so it thrives in a hydroponic system. Trim and harvest it weekly once it is mature. You can enjoy basil with many dishes and salads.

- **Anise**: Anise seeds and leaves provide a licorice taste. This can be useful in salads, flavor confections, and as a garnish. Anise plants grow rapidly from the seed to about 1–2 feet in height. A month after the anise blooms, the seeds can be gathered, used, and re-planted.

- **Chamomile**: Everyone loves chamomile tea as it not only tastes good but also has medicinal properties. This herb grows suitably in a soilless culture and takes only 6–12 weeks before you can fully enjoy the benefits.

- **Chives**: These herbs require minimal space to grow and tolerate various kinds of growing conditions so they will easily adapt in a hydroponic system. You will enjoy chives as a seasoning for main dishes and salads, as they are very aromatic.

- **Catnip**: This herb grows well whether in partial shade or full sun. A perennial that can grow up to 3–5 feet in height, will flourish well in a hydroponic system. You can propagate the catnip through seeds, root ball, or stem cutting.

- **Cilantro**: The cilantro will endure various conditions of pH and light, needs very little maintenance and you can harvest it in 6 weeks. It is a perfect herb to grow hydroponically. Once mature, trim regularly.

- **Chervil**: You have to remember that chervils require low lighting and cool temperatures. You need to set up your hydroponics system where there is shade and special cooling. You can harvest chervils in just 4 weeks. It is best to grow this herb during winter.

- **Dill**: Dill is a flavorful hydroponic herb that produces new growth every time you harvest it. You can make numerous cuttings from the lush growth of the compact leaf. It is best to replace the spent plants every 3–4 weeks so you have a continuous supply of dill.

- **Fennel**: Fennel looks like dill, with finely divided leaves. This herb may grow from seed to about 3–4 feet in height. Fennel seeds are condiments and you can harvest them when ripened. You can eat the flower stalks and leaves in salads.

- **Mint**: Mint is mostly aquatic or semi-aquatic making hydroponic systems the perfect medium for growing the different varieties. Peppermint, orange mint, and spearmint are some of the mints that flourish in soilless culture.

- **Lavender**: Lavender is a fragrant herb that is also a decorative plant. Lavender is used to making oil, vinegar, and lavender water and as a perfume for linens and clothing. It can grow well in hydroponic environments.

- **Oregano**: You can use oregano leaves whether they are fresh or dried. They have medicinal properties and you can use them as a flavoring for pizza, Italian sauces, and meat such as lamb. You can stimulate its foliage when you cut back the flowers, but you need to replant them as soon as they become woody.

- **Marjoram**: Marjoram is another fragrant herb for flavoring meat dishes and dressings. This herb can be sown in flats or plugs. Then they are transplanted in hydroponic units. You can harvest 6–10 weeks after planting the seeds.

- **Parsley**: Parsley is well suited for hydroponic systems because of its long taproot. Make sure that your container is at least a foot deep so you can get the best growing result for this delicious herb.

- **Sage**: You can add sage to sausages and dressings. You can grow sage in a hydroponic environment, provided that the herbs get enough sunlight and are protected from the cold. Harvest sage leaves before they bloom and dry them in well-ventilated rooms, away from sunlight.

- **Rosemary**: The aromatic leaves of rosemary are used as a seasoning and can be manufactured to produce medicinal oil. The herb needs protection from cold temperatures and will thrive when placed under full sunlight.

- **Thyme**: This herb will grow well in almost any condition. It requires very minimal fertilization and will flourish in hydroponic systems, especially when it is planted in the early spring.

- **Tarragon**: While it is not aromatic until the tops and leaves are harvested, the tarragon is essential for seasonings. It has a sweet smell and the oils are quite fragrant.

Vegetables

Grow your own vegetables at home and enjoy the fact that they are organic and insecticide-free. Some of the vegetables that thrive in a hydroponic garden are the following: lettuce, artichokes, spinach, beans, cabbage, asparagus, beets, broccoli, Brussels sprouts, cauliflower, and peas. Leafy greens grow very well hydroponically and require less maintenance. You can also grow watercress indoors, making hydroponic systems a perfect choice to cultivate this low-growing perennial. Be sure to harvest it before the flower buds appear so it remains edible.

The following vegetables usually grow in soil, but you can cultivate them hydroponically: onions, carrots, potatoes, leeks, parsnips, radishes, and yams. Think carefully before you start planting any of these vegetables because they require extra care.

If you have the time and can exert the effort, you will enjoy growing them. Here are some veggie crops to avoid: Zucchini, summer squash, corn, and plants that vine. While they can be grown hydroponically, they will not be very practical when it comes to space. These crops can easily take too much space. Hydroponic garden systems should be compact.

Fruits

Hydroponic gardening lets you grow fruits all year round. Water-loving fruits such as grape, cantaloupe, tomatoes, blueberries, strawberries, and raspberries can be grown in a hydroponics system. Some farmers can even grow pineapples with this gardening system.

Flowers

Hydroponic gardening will allow you to grow flowers in large numbers. Most flowers do well in hydroponic culture. The challenge is that every plant has particular needs—this means that they cannot be mixed in one hydroponic unit. For example, roses need larger amounts of potassium compared to daisies. Some plants can grow simultaneously in one unit. You need to be knowledgeable and very careful in matching flower species, so they get the right nutrient mix.

Succulents are not a good choice for hydroponic gardening, as they grow better in dry conditions.

Conclusion

G ardening is one of the calmest and most calming hobbies. Most people work in their gardens and flowerbeds for hours. The greenhouse is one of the easiest ways to enjoy gardening. You will deal with your plants throughout the year with a greenhouse. Read about home greenhouses and how in your gardening you can get the most from them.

Which will you need in your backyard for a greenhouse? It will rely on what you expect to expand and how much you are prepared to spend. You get some very cheap greenhouse kits while you also have a greenhouse installed to your specifications and pay for it a little more.

Where should you start learning everything about home greenhouses? The first place to look is on the Internet. There are many websites dedicated to greenhouse planting, while some are specialized in greenhouses. This way, you will find plenty of details or visit a kindergarten that sells greenhouses.

There are different kinds of greenhouses available for your home. A greenhouse kit is available. If you just start in your greenhouse hobby, this is a good way to go. These are also available online. You will be able to build your greenhouse and learn all about home greenhouses with these kits. You can get a pack for it, no matter what size you choose.

Greenhouses come in many sizes and shapes. Each is unique in its way and is suitable for the kind of plants you wish to grow. There are those designed for beginners and those made for the professional gardener. Whatever you choose will decide what you plan to grow and how you use a greenhouse will ultimately determine your buying.

If you choose one, you will want a robust greenhouse. You certainly don't want it to fly through the yard with high winds in the first storm. Make sure you select a reputable dealer and search in your greenhouse for some standard construction designs.

Make sure the greenhouse you choose has a lot of ventilation windows and is made long-lasting. You can usually choose models that are more inexpensive manually, or you can choose models that move up and down like house windows. All ventilation windows must have screens to avoid insects attacking you and your plants during the warmer months.

A portable greenhouse may be of interest to you. It's great for children who are interested in planting and watching things grow. This is also a good choice for people who rent their homes. When you pass, your greenhouse will easily be packed to go with you. The portable greenhouses are as effective as any other kind of greenhouse effect.

Were you aware that you could garden in your high-rise apartment on the veranda? If you want a lawn, but you felt you couldn't because you live in an apartment in town, you're in to have a treat. The indoor greenhouses are available to you. Both models are smaller than the larger ones and serve almost the same function and operate very well. These are great for the smaller courtyard gardens.

There are a couple of things you need to know about home greenhouses. You will need to learn a few supplies required to grow in a greenhouse. It's kind of like getting your house furniture. The first thing you will need for your new greenhouse is a table for plants. You will use any form of outdoor table or you can choose one provided by your greenhouse dealer.

Pot and flats holding your plants can be found in any kindergarten. Most of the plants you buy already come with your own. However, you will need all the supplies necessary if you are to start plants from seeds.

Combine a range of several potting soils. You will also need other forms of fertilizer for the plants you expect to grow. You can get tips on this in your local kindergarten or online.

The tools you need to learn about greenhouses will be relevant. You will need some small shovels and truffles in a greenhouse for your gardening activities. You'll also need gloves. Many soils and fertilizers can be pleasant on your skin, and some flowering plants such as roses do not have thorns.

Don't forget that you're going to need a greenhouse heater when it gets old outside. An outdoor greenhouse can be gardened throughout the year. A variety of heater models are available, which are only designed to heat a greenhouse. Normally, you will buy them for the same dealer you purchased your greenhouse.

There is a method available called hydroponics to those of you who know a bit about gardening in a greenhouse or even to those who still learn all about home greenhouses. This is a kind of cultivation that allows plants to grow like minerals and supplements in just water. No soil is used in a hydroponic cultivation process. This is a very popular way of growing plants in a greenhouse and was found to make crops like tomatoes and peppers very effective.

There is a lot to learn about home greenhouses, and you will learn much when you work in one yard. The fun of a greenhouse is to experiment and learn what you can and cannot grow.

Printed in Great Britain
by Amazon

78096140R00071